FOUNDATIONS 101

FOUNDATIONS 101

How to Start and Run a Great Foundation

STEPHEN L. ISAACS AND PAUL S. JELLINEK

Founding Partners
Isaacs/Jellinek
www.isaacs-jellinek.com

ISBN-13: **9781541177154**
ISBN-10: **1541177150**
Library of Congress Control Number: **2016921191**
CreateSpace Independent Publishing Platform
North Charleston, South Carolina

TABLE OF CONTENTS

Preface: Why We Wrote This Book

PREFACE: WHY WE WROTE THIS BOOK

After many years of working for and with foundations, we both believe in the remarkable potential of foundations to make the world a better place. Yet we also know from our experience in the field that foundations don't always live up to that potential. About fifteen years ago, the two of us met over lunch in San Francisco and formed a partnership dedicated to helping foundations achieve their full potential. Since then, as the founding partners of Isaacs/Jellinek, we have consulted with many foundations—as well as foundation-funded organizations—on everything from basic governance and management issues to strategic planning, program development and evaluation, impact assessment, and other challenges that foundations face as they strive to make a difference.

We have worked with both new and established foundations. Some were small and local in scope; others were large and had a regional or national focus. We've worked with foundations in cities, suburbs, and rural areas all over the country. Some were effectively managed, while others, shall we say, had problems. Along the way, we've helped foundation leaders deal with many of the issues that come up in the world of philanthropy. This book distills what we've learned in our more than fifty years of combined experience as grant makers, grantees, and consultants to foundations.

What distinguishes this book from the information available online is that it concisely sets out, in one place, just about everything that founders, directors, and CEOs and other staff members of foundations need to know in order to have a strong, effective foundation. This includes not only the technical aspects, such as obtaining the appropriate designation from the Internal Revenue Service, developing mission and vision statements, recruiting a CEO and staff, deciding on the foundation's grant-making priorities, and developing realistic strategies to achieve those priorities, but also—and every bit as important—non-technical insights that we've gleaned from our many years in the field about what it takes to become a great foundation. In an effort to maximize its usefulness, we have kept this book short and practical, avoided jargon wherever possible, and used real-life examples from our experience.

A word about our experience...

Stephen Isaacs, JD: I'm an attorney, writer-editor, and retired Columbia University professor of public health. Prior to becoming a partner in Isaacs/Jellinek, I spent more than 25 years as a program officer with U.S. Agency for International Development; vice president of the International Planned Parenthood Federation/Western Hemisphere Region; director of the Development Law and Policy Program and co-director of the International Women's Rights Action Watch at Columbia University; and president of the Center for Health and Social Policy. In addition to philanthropy, my areas of expertise include health, human rights, civil society, family planning, and socio-economic development—both international and domestic. Between 1997 and 2015, I co-edited *To Improve Health and Health Care: The Robert Wood Johnson Foundation Anthology*, a book series published by Jossey-Bass examining that foundation's programs and what could be learned from them. I'm the co-author of the best-selling book, *The Consumer's Legal Guide to Today's Health Care*, and I've written and edited books on tobacco control, community health, nursing, school health, palliative care, population policy, and Latin American health and development, among other topics. I've written for publications ranging from the *Chronicle of Philanthropy* and the *American Prospect* to the *Harvard International Law Journal* and the *New England Journal of Medicine*. A graduate of Brown University and Columbia Law School, I also serve as a director/trustee of The Royce Funds, a family of mutual funds.

Paul Jellinek, PhD: I came to the Isaacs/Jellinek partnership after nearly twenty years with the Robert Wood Johnson Foundation, the last eleven as a program vice president. By the time I left the foundation in 2002, I was responsible for a grant portfolio of $370 million in fields ranging from the health and safety of children to volunteer care for homebound elderly and disabled persons, as well as substance abuse prevention and treatment, access to health care, and community health. I was also an active board member of Grantmakers In Health. Since leaving the Robert Wood Johnson Foundation, in addition to the work that I've done with Stephen Isaacs, I have conducted an evaluation of a national nursing initiative of the Robert Wood Johnson Foundation and the Northwest Health Foundation (published in *Health Affairs*); written an internal history of the Kansas Health Foundation's grantmaking; co-authored a retrospective analysis of the David and Lucile Packard Foundation's work on children's health insurance (published online by the *Stanford Social Innovation Review*); and advised Children's Futures in its effort to improve the life chances of young children in Trenton, New Jersey. I hold bachelor's degrees from the University of Pennsylvania and the University of South Florida, and a doctorate in health policy and administration from the University of North Carolina School of Public Health, with a concentration in health economics. I've authored or co-authored articles for publications such as the *Chronicle of Philanthropy, Health Affairs*, the *Journal of Commerce*, and the *New England Journal of Medicine*, and drawing on some earlier experience in journalism, I've written several books, including *Promise to Mary*, which tells the story of the $75 million Faith in Action program that I started while at the Robert Wood Johnson Foundation.

A word about the structure of this book...

In the first section of *Foundations 101* (pages 1-22), we try to give the reader a clear understanding of what foundations are, why they are unique, and what options beyond foundations are available for philanthropically minded individuals of means. The middle and longest section of the book (pages 23-63) provides a practical guide through the various steps that need to be taken to establish and run a great foundation. In the final section (pages 65-73), we offer our judgment on what it takes to be a great foundation—which ultimately, we believe, has more to do with the foundation's culture and attitudes than with policies and procedures. Finally, we've included a list of websites, books, and journals that readers can turn to for additional information.

We hope that this book will be as enjoyable for you to read as it was for us to write, and that it will give those of you who are starting, overseeing, or running a foundation the basic knowledge and tools you'll need to help your foundation achieve its full potential.[*]

Stephen L. Isaacs and Paul S. Jellinek
February 2017

---

[*] We are immensely grateful to the following people for their insights as we crafted this book: Mary Backley, Andy Burness, Bruce Chernof, Adam Coyne, Susan Dentzer, Harvey Fineberg, Robert Hughes, Ilan Isaacs, Lauren Katzowitz, Peter Long, Faith Mitchell, David Morse, Steven Schroeder, Susan Zepeda, and Michael Ziegler. Their thoughtful guidance enabled us to improve the book at every stage.

FOUNDATIONS: A BRIEF HISTORY

Back in 1889, Andrew Carnegie published an article entitled *The Gospel of Wealth*, in which he argued that very wealthy people (like him) should devote their surplus wealth to philanthropic purposes—that is, to those purposes with the potential to "produce the most beneficial results for the community." About two decades later, in 1911, he set up America's first foundation, the Carnegie Corporation of New York. Among its other accomplishments, the Carnegie Corporation helped build the nation's system of public libraries. Not to be outdone, in 1913, John D. Rockefeller, arguably the richest man in modern history, established his own foundation that, among *its* accomplishments, brought about the Green Revolution that transformed agriculture worldwide and has been credited with saving over a billion lives.

Other wealthy Americans followed suit. In 1917, Julius Rosenwald, who made a fortune as president and part owner of Sears Roebuck, established a foundation that funded the construction of more than 5,000 schools—widely considered the most important initiative to advance African-American education in the early twentieth century. In 1936, Edsel Ford and his father Henry Ford endowed the Ford Foundation, which went on to play a leadership role in civil rights, urban redevelopment, and women's health. By the middle of the twentieth century, it had become accepted for men of great wealth to establish foundations, often bearing their names alone or in combination with their wives—foundations such as The John D. and Catherine T. MacArthur Foundation, known for its "genius awards;" the Robert Wood Johnson Foundation, the largest private funder of health programs in the United States; and the W. K. Kellogg Foundation, which has made improving children's wellbeing a priority.

More recently, spurred by the fortunes accruing to successful entrepreneurs, particularly in technology, the tradition has continued and even expanded. The Bill and Melinda Gates Foundation, the nation's largest foundation by far with an endowment of more than $40 billion, has invested substantially in efforts to wipe out diseases such as malaria in developing countries, as well as in education reform here in the United States. The William and Flora Hewlett Foundation and the David and Lucile Packard Foundation employ their multi-billion dollar endowments, among other ways, to protect the environment and slow climate change.

All told, there are now 86,000 foundations in the United States, with combined assets of nearly three-quarters of a trillion (with a *t*) dollars. They come in all shapes and sizes—including a vast array of relatively small local and family foundations—and they have an extraordinary potential to advance the public good in ways that neither government nor business can. Yet they are nearly invisible to most Americans.

WHAT MAKES FOUNDATIONS SPECIAL?

Foundations are a unique and powerful resource for the public good. One reason is that they have a lot of money to give away. If their resources are used wisely and effectively, foundations have the financial capacity to make a difference in improving people's lives—whether it is The Rockefeller Foundation trying to advance rural electrification in the developing world; the Cone Health Foundation working to gain support for Medicaid expansion in North Carolina; or the Ottumwa Regional Legacy Foundation striving to bring back a southeastern Iowa city that has gone through hard times.[†]

While the money *is* important, it is their independence that makes foundations unique. Foundations are responsible only to their boards of directors. They are generally not subject to

---

[†] Some foundations, like The Rockefeller Foundation, capitalize the T in "The"; others—like the Ottumwa Regional Legacy Foundation—don't. We have tried to follow each foundation's individual preferences.

outside review or challenge (although, in some cases, federal or state regulators do keep an eye on particular foundations). Unlike many businesses, which can be slaves to quarterly earnings reports, and unlike government, whose officials often want quick results that will please voters and increase their chances of re-election, foundations are able to take the long view. Their independence allows foundations to take risks that others cannot and to stick with programs—even those that don't appear to be succeeding at first—for many years. And it enables them to move quickly when the need to do so arises.

These are great strengths, but there is a very real downside risk: without outside scrutiny and accountability and without the competitive pressures of the market or the electoral process, it is all too easy for foundations to sink into complacency, and even mediocrity. For even if a foundation takes very few risks and implements its programs poorly, board members will continue serving and staff members will continue to be paid. Moreover, not many on the outside will be willing to run the risk of biting the hand that feeds them (or might one day feed them) by sharing any constructive criticisms or concerns they may have with the foundation. Consequently, how well a foundation does in achieving its true potential ultimately depends almost entirely on the personal commitment, integrity, and competence of both its board and its staff.

WHAT ARE FOUNDATIONS AND WHAT DO THEY DO?

Simply stated, foundations are tax-exempt not-for-profit or-ganizations established under the law to advance the public good, mainly by making grants to other charitable organizations for scientific, educational, cultural, religious, or other altruistic purposes.‡ Their work encompasses practically the entire spectrum of benevolent human activity: from supporting the local arts council to improving early childhood education in America; from restoring Main Street to preserving biodiversity around the world. In size, foundations' endowments range from less than a million dollars to many billions. And while most foundations

---

‡ The term "foundation" has been used to describe a wide range of organizations. In this book, we will not be discussing those organizations that are called foundations but whose primary function is fund-raising (for example, disease-specific foundations such as the National Kidney Foundation and the National Foundation for Ectodermal Dysplasias, or the many local hospital foundations whose primary role is to raise money for their hospital) or any of the government agencies that are called foundations, such as the National Science Foundation and the Louisiana Wildlife and Fisheries Foundation.

are set up to last forever, a small minority of them have decided to spend all their assets and go out of business at a specified time. The multi-billion-dollar Atlantic Philanthropies, for example, is set to go out of business in just a few years and is in the process of making its final grants. The Gates Foundation has announced that it will spend down all of its assets within twenty years after the death of Bill and Melinda Gates.

Although they come in so many varieties that it is often said, "If you've seen one foundation, you've seen one foundation," foundations can be best understood when considered in terms of three basic characteristics: (1) how they are structured, (2) whose money is behind them, and (3) what they do.

Understanding Foundations by Their Legal Structure and its Consequences

The U.S. Internal Revenue Service, which determines a foundation's legal status, has set up two classifications of foundations under section 501(c)(3) of the Internal Revenue Code: private foundations and public charities. Each is treated somewhat differently under the law.

Private Foundations

The first, and most common, classification is a *private foundation*. Private foundations must spend at least 5 percent of their endowment annually for charitable purposes or face a penalty levied by the IRS.

They are also subject to a 1 or 2 percent excise tax on investment income. The tax aspects of private foundations can be quite complex; it requires the services of an experienced attorney to navigate them.

An important point to note about private foundations: in 1968, alarmed by allegations that some foundations were using their funds to influence elections and to lobby legislators, Congress passed a law that prohibited private foundations from supporting candidates for public office and placed strict limits on the amount of lobbying they can do. For foundations wishing to influence public policy, this can appear to be a daunting obstacle. Many private foundations, however, have found ways to engage in the policy process within the limits imposed by Congress by funding activities such as policy research, advocacy, and the education of policy makers and the public.

Operating Foundations

Operating foundations, a sub-category of private foundations, carry out their charitable work themselves, rather than delegating it to others through their grant making. The Henry J. Kaiser Family Foundation, for example, was for many years an operating foundation that used its own staff to conduct policy analyses and shared health policy information widely through its website and the media (it recently became a public charity). Another prominent operating foundation is the Howard Hughes Medical Institute, which employs more than 2,500 scientists and other individuals across the country to conduct biomedical research. Operating foundations do not have the same 5 percent distribution requirement as other private foundations; their payout is

Stephen L. Isaacs and Paul S. Jellinek

the lesser of their adjusted net income or minimum investment return.

Public Charities

To gain and maintain *public charity* status, a foundation must raise a substantial share of its support from the public. A foundation seeking public charity status must meet one of two tests: either it must raise a third of its support from contributions from the public or it must meet a "facts and circumstances test," which requires the foundation to raise at least 10 percent of its support from the public. The tests are complicated; the services of a good attorney will be needed to guide a foundation through the regulatory thicket. Passing the public support test is difficult for foundations created by an individual donor or family, although some, such as The Pew Charitable Trusts, have successfully done so. Unlike private foundations, public charities do not have a 5 percent payout requirement, and they are allowed to lobby.

Another way to gain public charity status is to become a *supporting organization*—that is, an organization that aids the work of an existing 501(c)(3) organization or organizations. The Cone Health Foundation in Greensboro, North Carolina, for example, furthers the community work of Cone Health, a non-profit healthcare delivery system, and is therefore classified as a supporting organization. The Foundation for a Healthy Kentucky qualifies as a supporting organization because it supports all of the state's nonprofit organizations working to address the unmet health needs of Kentuckians.

Unless a foundation can meet the public support test either by raising a substantial proportion of its support from the public or by becoming a supporting organization, the IRS will classify it as a private foundation.

501(c)(4) Organizations

To avoid the limitations on lobbying, foundations wishing to play a substantial role in public policy can register with the IRS as a 501(c)(4) corporation. Though it may act like and be called a foundation, a 501(c)(4) organization is, according to the IRS, a *social welfare organization*. The California Health Care Foundation and the Missouri Foundation for Health are examples of 501(c)(4) organizations. 501(c)(4) organizations are not subject to the 5 percent distribution requirement; they do not have to disclose their donors publicly; they are allowed to lobby and, subject to some limitations, to engage in political activity. Donations to them are not tax deductible.

Limited Liability Corporations (LLCs)

In a December 2015 letter to their newborn daughter, Mark Zuckerberg and his wife Priscilla Chan announced their plans to dedicate 99 percent of their Facebook shares, then valued north of $40 billion, to "improving this world for the next generation." Rather than setting up a foundation through which to channel their charitable endeavors, they took the unusual step of establishing an LLC, called the Chan Zuckerberg Initiative, to which they plan to transfer their Facebook stock over a period of years. The Initiative will, in turn, fund nonprofit organizations, make private investments, and participate in policy debates. Under this philanthropic structure, Zuckerman and Chan presumably forgo the immediate tax benefits of a charitable contribution to a foundation but retain complete control over how the money is spent. It also frees them from the requirement of spending 5 percent of the assets on charitable activities each year and permits them to lobby.

The Zuckerman-Chan approach is not the first of its kind. Other West Coast entrepreneurs have also employed it. For instance, eBay founder Pierre Omidyar set up the Omidyar Network, which has taken a hybrid approach by operating as both an LLC and a nonprofit. Writing in *The Harvard Business Review*, Omidyar explained his motivation: "In thinking about philanthropy, I began looking for ways to harness the incredible power of business in order to make the world better… We were breaking new ground here—our attorneys had never seen a structure like this. Today there's a name for people who make investments that can produce both impact and profit: impact investors."

Whether LLCs and similar corporate structures will turn out to be the wave of the future or merely a flash in pan, only time will tell.

Understanding Foundations by Their Founders

Another way to understand foundations is by looking at who gave the money to start them.

Family Foundations

Building on the example set by Andrew Carnegie and John D. Rockefeller, an increasing number of financially successful people have chosen to establish *family foundations*. While more than 70 percent of the roughly 40,000 family foundations have endowments of less than $10 million, there are some notable exceptions, such as the Walton Family Foundation, with an endowment of $2.2 billion. The National Center for Family Philanthropy represents larger family foundations, and Exponent Philanthropy serves as a resource for family foundations with few or no staff members.

Community Foundations

As an alternative to establishing their own personal foundation, individuals and families can contribute to a *community foundation*, which pools the combined resources of its donors but still allows individual donors to direct how their money will be used. There are now more than 700 community foundations throughout the United States. The New York Community Trust, one of the nation's largest community foundations, pools more than

2,000 different charitable funds in its $2.5 billion endowment. Perhaps more typical is the Emporia Community Foundation in Emporia, Kansas, with assets of roughly $17 million.

Conversion or Legacy Foundations

Under the law, the assets of a nonprofit corporation that is bought by or "converted" into a for-profit corporation must continue to be used for non-profit purposes generally similar to those of the original organization. One common way of complying with this legal requirement is to use the assets to establish a new foundation. Beginning in the 1980s, as nonprofit hospitals and health insurers, including state and local Blue Cross Blue Shield organizations, were acquired by for-profit organizations, a large number—more than 300 at last count—of *conversion foundations*, sometimes called *legacy foundations*, was created with the assets. While many of them have endowments of less than $100 million, some, such as the Missouri Foundation for Health (endowment of roughly $1 billion) and The California Endowment (endowment of more than $3 billion), are quite substantial. Another source of funds for legacy foundations derives from the settlement of lawsuits. The Physicians Foundation, for example, was created from the proceeds of the settlement of a lawsuit brought by state and county medical societies against health insurance companies, and the American Legacy Foundation (now Truth Initiative) was established from the settlement of a lawsuit by attorneys general of 46 states against the major tobacco companies.

Corporate Foundations

As part of what is considered their responsibility to the communities they serve, large companies sometimes set up a *corporate foundation*, such as the Pfizer Foundation or the Walmart Foundation. With close ties to the parent company, a corporate foundation's grant making is often designed to further the company's interests or to enhance its reputation, as well as serving the public good. For instance, the Levi Strauss Foundation, with its corporate headquarters in San Francisco, gives particular attention to social justice in the Bay Area; it also funds human rights and social development projects in other places where it does business.

Understanding Foundations by What They Do

Not surprisingly, the nation's 86,000 foundations work on all kinds of topics—everything from promoting free enterprise to supporting the local women's shelter; from halting nuclear proliferation to fostering the spread of community gardens. Often, a foundation may be making grants in many of these areas at the same time. The Gordon and Betty Moore Foundation, for example, lists four distinct priority areas: scientific discovery, environmental conservation, improvements in patient care, and preservation of the special character of the San Francisco Bay Area.

Increasingly worried that they may be spreading themselves too thin, many foundations have chosen to concentrate on a limited number of issues. Foundations with priorities in the same area sometimes belong to associations that allow them to interact with and learn from each other, and that can represent their interests in Washington. Thus, another way of understanding foundations is by their area of concentration. Examples include:

Foundations focused on health, such as the Health Foundation of South Florida, The REACH Healthcare Foundation, The Commonwealth Fund, and the Robert Wood Johnson Foundation. Grantmakers In Health serves their interests.

Foundations focused on education, such as The Grable Foundation, the Lumina Foundation, and The Wallace Foundation. Grantmakers for Education serves their interests.

Foundations focused on the elderly, such as The Retirement Research Foundation, The Harry and Jeanette Weinberg Foundation, The John A. Hartford Foundation, and The SCAN Foundation. Grantmakers in Aging serves their interests.

Foundations focused on the arts, either giving it their exclusive focus, such as the Bonfils-Stanton Foundation and the Andy Warhol Foundation, or a substantial focus, such as the Howard Gilman Foundation, the Ahmanson Foundation, and the Hemera Foundation. Grantmakers in the Arts serves their interests.

Foundations focused on young people, such as the Annie E. Casey Foundation, the William T. Grant Foundation, and the W.K. Kellogg Foundation.

Foundations focused on the environment, either exclusively, such as the Bullitt Foundation and the Brainerd Foundation, or as an important priority, such as the Charles Stewart Mott Foundation, The Pew Charitable Trusts, and the John D. and Catherine T. MacArthur Foundation. The Environmental Grantmakers Association serves their interests.

The Council on Foundations, The Independent Sector, The Philanthropy Roundtable, and Grantmakers for Effective Organizations, as well as regional associations of grant makers, serve the interests of foundations as a whole.

THE PROS AND CONS OF STARTING A FOUNDATION

For wealthy people who want to contribute in a meaningful way to improving society, starting a foundation can be an excellent option. By establishing a foundation, the donor is creating a potentially powerful new organization with resources of its own that can actively pursue whatever social purpose or vision the donor chooses, both during and after the donor's lifetime, in most cases in perpetuity. A donor who has a passion for, say, preventing diabetes can make sure that the foundation remains 100 percent focused on that goal, now and in the future. An engaged living donor—such as a Bill Gates or a George Soros—can also determine how the foundation operates. For example, such a donor can see to it that the foundation's funds are allocated to high-risk or innovative approaches—something that he or she could not do by simply donating to an existing organization—and can insist that the foundation hire a top-flight staff with the charge to think boldly. A donor can also insist that the foundation be flexible in carrying out its programs and learning from its experiences. Thanks to these advantages, a foundation offers donors the potential to have a big impact in an area of importance to them.

Moreover, establishing a foundation is an effective way to create an enduring legacy for the founder and his or her family, and can be a way of involving one's children and future generations in the family's philanthropic activities. It also carries significant tax advantages. Donors can deduct up to 30 percent of their adjusted gross income for cash donations and up to 20 percent of appreciated property.

There are, however, some downsides. Foundations can be time-consuming and costly to establish and operate. Starting a foundation generally requires the services of an attorney experienced in philanthropy, and it usually takes a good deal of time (and expense) just to complete the paperwork necessary to comply with state and federal requirements. With the exception of the very smallest foundations, setting up a foundation also involves recruiting a board, which then must hire a CEO, who in turn hires a staff to do the actual work of the foundation. And as we discussed earlier, a private foundation must pay out 5 percent of its endowment each year to support charitable activities, plus a 1 or 2 percent excise tax on investment income. In addition, the IRS requires time-consuming financial reporting on a Form 990.

For those who want to avoid these headaches, there are tax-advantaged options other than foundations available to wealthy people who want to give back. They can simply donate to charities of their choice, such as the Red Cross, the local symphony, or the

National Wildlife Federation. Or they can establish a donor-advised fund with a charitable trust or a community foundation. Both pool the contributions of donors, invest the money, and spend it on the organizations or activities that the donors designate. Banks and financial management firms such as Fidelity and Schwab establish and administer charitable trusts. Community foundations such as the Greater Kansas City Community Foundation or the San Francisco Foundation do the same. We should note that although the wishes of the donors are followed nearly all the time, the final decisions are those of the institutions administering the trust or community foundation. From a tax perspective, charitable trusts and community foundations offer greater tax advantages than do private foundations. Cash contributions can be deducted up to 50 percent of the donor's adjusted gross income, and appreciated securities and real property up to 30 percent.

Establishing a foundation offers donors control of how their funds will be spent, assures a legacy, and provides an opportunity to have a real impact. But it is expensive and time-consuming. Contributing to a charitable trust or community foundation avoids the cost and hassle of running a foundation, while still allowing donors the chance to support a cause they believe in. But donors lose both the absolute control of how their money will be spent and the prestige that comes from having a foundation. All the alternatives have tax advantages; those for contributing to a charitable trust or community foundation are greater than those for contributing to a private foundation.

For the vast majority of people with sufficient wealth and a social conscience, we believe that the tried-and-true choices of starting a foundation or, alternatively, setting up a donor-advised fund with a community foundation or charitable trust will be the logical choices. However, as we discussed earlier, there are other options—including 501(c)(4) social welfare organizations, limited liability corporations, and other kinds of hybrid entities—that may be worth exploring.

In any case, anybody thinking about starting a foundation—or choosing one of the alternatives—should consult with a financial expert and/or attorney. They should carefully consider their and their families' needs and wishes, their long-range goals, the tax implications, what they want to accomplish, the time frame for accomplishing it, and the amount of money they have available to contribute for charitable purposes. As a rule of thumb, donors planning to start a foundation should be willing to contribute at least $5 million to it.

STARTING AND RUNNING A GREAT FOUNDATION

> "The distribution of money judiciously is not
> without its difficulties... and involves harder
> work than ever acquisition of wealth did."

ANDREW CARNEGIE

Initial Steps: From Incorporation to Hiring a CEO

The first step in setting up a new foundation is for the founders to articulate an early vision—perhaps even an aspirational sketch about what they hope the foundation will accomplish, but in any case something that can provide general guidance to the initial board and future boards about the founders' intentions.

The next steps are inevitably legal ones, as is true in establishing any new company. Legal requirements vary from state to state. Consequently, as we have suggested, finding a good, experienced lawyer is an early priority. With the guidance of an attorney, there is a relatively standard checklist of steps that have to be taken in order to get the foundation up and running. Specifically, those responsible for establishing the foundation must:

Draft articles of incorporation and submit them to the state

The charter, as articles of incorporation are sometimes called, is a legal document that, among other things, spells out the purposes of the foundation and what its limits are. It will likely incorporate the founders' vision.

In the case of a conversion foundation, the state attorney general or other government officials may be involved. This can sometimes be contentious. In a transaction that was completed in 2003, the Hospital Corporation of America (HCA) bought Health Midwest, a hospital system based in Kansas City. The attorneys general of the two states in which Kansas City lies—Missouri and Kansas—oversaw the sale and reached an agreement that two health foundations should be established with the assets. The REACH Healthcare Foundation received 20 percent of the proceeds (roughly $100 million) and The Health Care Foundation of Greater Kansas City received 80 percent (about $400 million).

Select a board of directors

The importance of choosing a strong board—and board chair—cannot be overstated. In the case of family foundations, their boards generally include family members but may also include non-family members to provide expertise or perspectives not represented among the family members themselves. While most foundations do not compensate board members, some provide an honorarium for their time and service.

In the case of conversion foundations, the attorney general or another government body may set out requirements for board membership. This has led to the creation of unusual boards, as occurred in New York. Under the legislation authorizing its establishment, The New York State Health Foundation was required to have a board comprised of three members selected by the State Senate, three members selected by the State Assembly, and three members selected by the Governor. This could easily have resulted in a foundation characterized by patronage grants to political favorites or by feuding among board members of different parties. Fortunately, the board did not fall into partisan traps, and the foundation's CEO insisted that the foundation's processes be aboveboard and transparent. As a result, the foundation became widely respected throughout New York State as fair and impartial.

Apply to the IRS for an Employer Identification Number and 501(c)(3) status

As discussed earlier, the foundation could be established as a public charity or a private foundation, depending on its intended purpose and its ability to meet the public support test.

Adopt bylaws

The bylaws set out how the foundation will be governed and contain, among other provisions: the number of board members, their length of service, and how often the board meets; the committees of the board and their functions; the number and function of officers of the board; and what constitutes a conflict of interest.

Appoint the foundation's officers

These generally include the president, vice president, secretary, and treasurer.

Appoint committees

Although these vary from foundation to foundation, they often include an executive committee, an audit committee, a nominating committee, a grants or program committee, and an investment committee. Many conversion foundations also have a community advisory committee comprised of community members not on the board.

Find and hire a chief executive officer

This is probably the most important early function of the board. In the past, most CEOs were called executive directors; today they are commonly given the title of president. The CEO—who is, of course, accountable to the board—is the public face of the foundation and the liaison between staff and board. It is the CEO who recommends policies and programs to the board; hires (and, when necessary, fires) staff; and, broadly speaking, is the leader of the foundation.

It can take months—and sometimes as much as a year or more—to recruit a CEO. Most sizeable foundations hire a recruiting firm to identify, screen, and recommend qualified candidates. Once the list of candidates is winnowed down to three or four, the board can interview the finalists and make its selection. In exercising its fiduciary responsibility and trying to conserve the foundation's assets, a board will sometimes make the mistake of setting the CEO's pay at too low a level to attract the most qualified candidate. It is important to remember that, as with most organizations, the quality of leadership provided by the CEO is generally the single most important determinant of the foundation's effectiveness and impact. Consequently, setting the CEO's compensation below the level needed to attract and retain a first-rate candidate may well prove to be penny-wise and pound-foolish.

Next Steps: Once the CEO is Hired

Once the CEO is in place, a number of actions need to be taken over a relatively brief period of time:

Establish a strong working relationship between the board and staff

This is something that evolves over time, but to get things off on the right foot, a few simple guidelines should be kept in mind:

- **The board must step back**

  Everything changes when a CEO is hired. In the period prior to the CEO's taking office, boards can get used to being in charge. They sometimes find it hard to let go, and, as a result, tend to micro-manage. Not only does this practice lead to morale problems, but it undermines the role of the staff.

- **Delineate board-staff roles and relationships as clearly as possible**

  These roles are easy enough to state: boards have a fiduciary responsibility to govern the foundation, while the staff, under the guidance of the board, is responsible for managing the organization and carrying out the work. But adhering to these roles in practice may not be so easy. Much depends on individual personalities, on the extent and nature of communication between the CEO and the board, and on the community context. We have seen cases where the board exercises very tight control, leaving the CEO as something of a figurehead. This happens most commonly in family foundations, where family members can easily dominate the board. In other cases, a strong CEO can overshadow the board—remember that board members usually serve for a limited period and meet just a few times a year, while the CEO gives full time to the foundation and is therefore far better informed than the board. In our experience, neither a domineering board nor a domineering staff is in the best interest of the foundation.

- **Develop clear lines of communication between the CEO and the board**

We advise foundations that, except in emergencies, the CEO and board chair should meet in person on at least a monthly basis, and if there is an executive committee, the CEO should meet with it prior to board meetings. The executive committee should know about, and bless, anything of importance being brought to the board. There are few things worse for the leadership of a board than being blindsided by an unexpected announcement or controversial proposal at a board meeting. In addition, if possible, the CEO should periodically meet informally with each individual board member as a way to share perspectives and foster mutual understanding.

Name the foundation

A foundation's name should be easy to remember and should give some idea of what it does, where it is located, or who established it. Foundations established by individuals, families, and companies are simple: the name of the donor plus "Foundation"—thus, the Nathan Cummings Foundation or The SCAN Foundation. Similarly, community foundations are a no-brainer: the name of the community plus "Foundation" or "Trust"—for example, the Cleveland Foundation or The New York Community Trust. Naming a conversion or legacy foundation sometimes takes a little more effort, as it may involve both the location and an indicator about what it does—for example, The California Wellness Foundation and the Kansas Health Foundation.

Determine the organization's structure and staffing

Unless it's very small, a foundation will need a staff to carry out the organization's functions. As mentioned earlier, the CEO is the key staff position. But a CEO is only one person and cannot do the job alone. Although every foundation will have different personnel needs, generally speaking, other key staff positions include the following:

- **Program officer or officers**

    Often the eyes and ears of the foundation in the community, program officers develop and oversee the foundation's programs, draft requests for proposals, review proposals, monitor the foundation's grantees, and serve as liaisons with grantees and others in the community. Larger foundations tend to have a hierarchy of program staff, including program vice presidents, senior program officers, program officers, program associates and program assistants. Grant-making foundations usually recruit program officers with advanced degrees and knowledge that will enable them to handle a wide variety of topics, although some foundations look for topic expertise. Operating foundations generally look for specialists in their field rather than generalists. Regardless of whether they are generalists or specialists, the best program officers get out of the office and into the field often, keep abreast of developments in their area and related areas, and interact as equals with grantees and potential grantees.

- **Grants manager**

An underappreciated but critical position, the grants manager is in charge of everything having to do with grants—which, after all, comprise the main business of most foundations. He or she screens grant applications, oversees due diligence of grantees, keeps track of grantees' expenditures, and provides reports on grants to the CEO and/or the board.

- **Finance officer/controller**

In small foundations, this position is sometimes combined with the grants manager. In medium-sized and larger foundations, the finance officer/controller handles and reports on the finances of the organization, including compliance with IRS regulations. In larger foundations, the financial staff may monitor grantee expenditures.

- **Communications officer**

  In addition to these key staff positions, many larger foundations choose to bring on a communications officer to manage external communications, including media relations, community relations, website development, and development of reports and other materials to be distributed to the public.

- **Human resources officer**

  Larger foundations often have a human resources officer to handle personnel and related matters.

- **Investment officer**

  Generally found in larger foundations, the person in this position either manages the foundation's investment portfolio directly or, more likely, monitors the work of an outside firm (or firms) that manages the foundation's investment portfolio.

- **Clerical staff**

  Administrative assistants or secretaries plan meetings, schedule travel for program staff members, answer the telephone, and carry out other clerical tasks.

Larger foundations are likely to require more than one individual to perform each of these functions and may therefore create multi-staff offices or departments in areas such as program development and management, grants management, finance, communications, investments, and human resources. They may also establish a separate evaluation and/or learning department, as well as an information technology unit or department.

Introduce the foundation to the community

Although it would seem that the infusion of new money aimed at advancing the public good would be welcome, that has not always proven to be the case. New foundations are sometimes met with skepticism that the money will be well spent or with concerns that the new foundation will play favorites. Community residents, upset about the loss of "their hospital," have greeted some conversion foundations with hostility. Whatever the facts behind a foundation's creation, it is important, as the former head of a conversion foundation with a troubled start told us, "to step out smartly and to garner community support quickly."

The obvious way to start is by talking with constituents and getting their views on what the needs are and what the foundation can do to address them. Although it doesn't necessarily have to be a formal "listening tour," such openness is likely to give the foundation credibility and allow its leaders to find out what the community expects of it. Moreover, it offers the foundation an opportunity to establish its identify. By defining itself at the outset, the foundation preempts others from defining it. This can help to build credibility and public support—support that may prove invaluable later on if the foundation takes a principled but unpopular stand on an issue or finds itself at odds with powerful vested interests.

How and when to introduce the foundation to the public will depend on the circumstances. For the most part, the creation of a new foundation and an infusion of new money will be viewed positively and should be announced quickly through press releases, social media posts, and interviews with the media. There is, however, an argument for delay. Broad publicity about a new source of money can raise expectations in the community and generate pressure to award funding before the foundation has decided what it is going to do.

To avoid raising expectations prematurely, it may be wise to keep a low profile until the foundation board has decided on its priorities and can award grants in a thoughtful way. If, however, the pressure to begin spending money becomes intense, a series of modest non-renewable grants to well-run community organizations may buy the foundation some additional time and do some good along the way.

Find appropriate offices

This is not as obvious as it might seem. Foundations can be pretty intimidating places, and the ostentatious offices of some foundation headquarters can be more than a little off-putting to potential grantees, especially those coming from low-budget community organizations. Indeed, such shows of wealth by organizations dedicated to charitable purposes are simply inappropriate and exacerbate the power differential between foundations and the communities they serve. Offices located in difficult-to-reach areas also send the wrong message: visitors and potential grantees are not welcome here.

The California Endowment, which was initially located in the relatively inaccessible Los Angeles suburb of Woodland Hills, moved its offices to a low-income, predominately minority area in downtown Los Angeles. It dedicated the first floor of its new facility to meeting space which community groups are welcome to use. Along the same lines, the Annie E. Casey Foundation, which focuses on children in poverty, moved its offices from the upscale New York City suburb of Greenwich, Connecticut, to an urban neighborhood in downtown Baltimore. And the Ford Foundation is currently converting its suite of offices in its luxurious East Side Manhattan office building into office and meeting space that is less formal and more community-friendly.

Find an investment advisor

To be able to make the required 5 percent payout and to cover the federal excise tax and administrative costs that cannot be included in the payout, the return on the foundation's investments must exceed 5 percent annually. And remember that 5 percent is the *minimum* payout required by law for private foundations. Some foundations, such as The California Wellness Foundation, have chosen to increase their payout above 5 percent during financial downturns in order to honor their existing commitments to their grantees; these foundations must earn a return considerably in excess of 5 percent or risk dipping into their endowment. Thus, finding a good investment advisor at the outset should be a high priority.

The first step is making sure that the board includes one or more members who understand finance and investments. If that capacity does not exist among the directors, then the board should constitute an advisory committee of individuals with the necessary expertise.

Although some large national foundations have in-house investment specialists, most look for outside expertise to manage their money. Fortunately, there is a cottage industry (actually, given the sums of money involved, it is more like a castle industry) of investment firms specializing in or knowledgeable about institutional investing. A request for proposals—either open or, more likely, to a selected group of potential investment advisors—will narrow the field. Generally, the investment committee or the entire board will interview three firms prior to selecting one as the foundation's investment counselor.

Set the foundation's priorities

Deciding what the foundation is actually going to do is clearly something that it should begin to address as soon as possible after the CEO comes on board. Since this is so important to a foundation's ultimate effectiveness and to the community that it serves, we deal with it at length in the following section.

Mission, Vision, and Values

Determining what the foundation is going to do is an initial and ongoing challenge. Some foundations choose to sprinkle their money around, funding many organizations in the community or in their chosen area of interest, such as the arts, the environment, or children's wellbeing. This allows those organizations to exist, and perhaps to thrive, in a way that might be difficult without foundation support. Other foundations believe they will have greater impact if they limit their focus.

Strategic foundations often find it useful to articulate a mission and/or a vision statement, and a values statement. These provide a framework within which the organization can articulate its priorities, set its goals, and develop a strategic plan to guide its grant making over a period of years (usually five years or longer).

> Mission, vision, and values statements define the very essence of a foundation: what it stands for, what it hopes to accomplish, and what principles it will adhere to.

Many foundations choose to ask outside consultants with expertise in philanthropy to provide assistance in developing these statements. In carrying out their assignment, consultants frequently will interview board and staff members, as well as community members and outside stakeholders, in an effort to understand what the foundation's leadership really wants and to distill their sentiments into a few well-chosen sentences.

A mission statement captures in a concise yet broad way what the foundation hopes to accomplish. Often the stuff of NPR tag lines, a mission statement sets the foundation's direction, serving as something of a North Star that staff, board, and outsiders can refer to.§ Here are some examples of mission statements:

"To reduce poverty and injustice, strengthen democratic values, promote international cooperation, and advance human achievement." (The Ford Foundation)

"To support creative people and effective institutions committed to building a more just, verdant, and peaceful world." (The John D. and Catherine T. MacArthur Foundation)

"To help individuals attain economic independence by advancing educational achievement and entrepreneurial success." (The Ewing Marion Kauffman Foundation)

A vision statement, which some foundations use to complement their mission statement, articulates what things will be

§ The articles of incorporation may establish the purposes of the foundation. The mission must be consistent with these.

like if the foundation is successful. Usually somewhat longer and more concrete than the mission, the vision statement is a brief description of the foundation's long-term aspirations, and even its dreams. Three examples of vision statements follow below:

"A society where older adults can access health and supportive services of their choosing to meet their needs." (The SCAN Foundation)

"As a nation, to strive together to build a Culture of Health enabling all in our diverse society to lead healthier lives, now and for generations to come." (The Robert Wood Johnson Foundation)

"We are guided by a vision of social justice—a world in which all individuals, communities, and peoples work toward the protection and full expression of their human rights; are active participants in the decisions that affect them; share equitably in the knowledge, wealth, and resources of society; and are free to achieve their full potential." (The Ford Foundation)

A statement of values or principles does just what the words suggest, and gives the staff and board a kind of moral compass to look to for guidance when confronted with difficult and perhaps unpopular decisions. Based on our experience with foundations, we know that values statements do, in fact, serve to guide board and staff members when they are faced with challenging situations. Here are two illustrations:

The Ottumwa Regional Legacy Foundation

* Courageous: We will be steadfast in our commitment to do what we believe is right, even in the face of opposition.
* Honest: We will be open and truthful in our dealings with others.
* Collaborative: We will seek to work with others to achieve our mission.
* Respectful: We will treat others with dignity and fairness.
* Trustworthy: We will be a dependable community resource, and honor our commitments.

The San Francisco Foundation

* Accountability: Taking responsibility for delivering on our mission.
* Integrity: Demonstrating integrity through accessible, timely, and responsive actions.
* Excellence: Fostering excellence and leadership in individuals and institutions.
* Social Justice: Addressing disparities and strengthening the rights and voices of the most vulnerable in our community.
* Leadership: Demonstrating proactive leadership on issues that are crucial to communities we serve.
* Diversity: Creating a culture of access, inclusion, and equity in all aspects of our work.

Strategic Planning

> Strategic planning does not need to be complicated. It doesn't have to rely on gimmicks or catchy theories.

Although it takes time and is hard to do well, developing a strategic plan is conceptually simple. It is essentially a four-step process: (1) assess the context and needs; (2) determine the resources available to meet them, including resources and tools outside of the foundation; (3) based on that assessment, set priorities and goals; and (4) develop strategies to reach the goals. It sounds very simple—perhaps overly so—but in practice, this framework allows a foundation to go into great depth. Based on our experience in helping foundations develop strategic plans, we share, below, a process that we have used successfully with many of our clients.

Step 1: Assess the context and needs

To develop a strategic plan, the foundation must first identify the context (political, social, economic) and the most pressing needs. There are a number of ways of doing this. It could:

- **Scan the community or field**

  This can be carried out through literature reviews, analysis of existing data or surveys, the fielding of new surveys if necessary, and focus group sessions with community members and leaders.

- **Conduct stakeholder interviews**

  As part of their research, foundations often interview stakeholders in order to get their perspective on the most pressing needs. This may include interviewing community leaders; business, non-profit, civic, and religious leaders; public officials; academics; journalists, and others.

  The Foundation for a Healthy Kentucky found an innovative way of unearthing issues: to supplement findings from a large-scale population survey and vital statistics data collected by the government, it hired an experienced analyst to go around the state and talk with a wide cross-section of residents (some identified by the foundation, others whom the interviewer met randomly in places like parks and truck stops). This quasi-journalistic approach revealed issues that a more formal survey or focus groups might have missed.

- **Interview board and staff members**

  As knowledgeable individuals and leaders of the foundation, the views and judgments of board and staff members are important. Interviews of the board and staff should reveal the issues that they truly care about. Although "passion" is not a word commonly associated with foundations, it can be critical if the foundation is to tackle tough issues and to stay with them for the long haul.

As an example, the president of the Cone Health Foundation in Greensboro, North Carolina, cares deeply about enabling the poor in Greensboro to gain access to affordable health care. Her passion led the foundation, as part of its strategic planning process, to redouble its effort to persuade reluctant state lawmakers to expand Medicaid—an effort that included funding a widely publicized study that documented the economic implications of Medicaid expansion for every county in the state and then publishing a strongly worded op-ed co-authored by the foundation's president and board chair.

- **Invite experts to weigh in**

  Bringing in knowledgeable outsiders can lend a valuable external perspective to the strategic planning process. They may be asked to prepare a report or, simply, to meet with staff members.

Step 2: Discover what resources and tools are available to address the needs

Resources

Foundations do not work in a vacuum. Particularly for foundations trying to bring about social change, it is important to know what other foundations, government agencies, the private sector, and non-profits are doing or planning to do. This allows a foundation to find its niche, as well as to identify potential partners.

In its strategic planning process, the Missouri Foundation for Health conducted a needs assessment and discovered not only that lack of access to dental care was a major problem for poor children in the state but also that few other funders were interested in addressing it. Accordingly, the foundation made oral health one of its priorities, funding the establishment of a community dentistry program via a partnership between a university and a St. Louis community health center, and partially paying for a newly restored position of state dental health director.

On the other hand, when the Community Foundation for the Land of Lincoln started working on nursing workforce issues in central Illinois, its staff discovered that a number of other community foundations and other organizations across the state were keenly interested in the same issues. As a result, what began as a regional partnership was greatly expanded and wound up having a statewide impact.

Tools

Foundations have a number of tools that they can deploy. **First and foremost, of course, they can award money to organizations working in the areas that the foundation has identified as important.** Although one sometimes hears in philanthropic circles that "it's not just the money," the fact is that the money *is* important—especially to struggling

nonprofit organizations. The money is almost always award-
ed as a grant to an organization that will, in accordance with
its agreement with the foundation, spend it on activities such
as demonstration programs, direct services, advocacy, research, policy analysis, or communications, as well as fellow-
ships, prizes, buildings, equipment, training, or technical
assistance. Foundations vary in what they will support. Some,
for example, exclude funding for buildings, endowments or
core support, while others encourage proposals for such
purposes.

A Note on "Impact Investing"

Some foundations attempt to merge philanthropy
with private enterprise principles through what is
called "impact investing," a name originally coined
by The Rockefeller Foundation. Impact investing is
generally carried out through two vehicles: program-
related investments (PRIs) and mission-related investments (MRIs). While these vehicles differ, the basic
premise is that a foundation sees itself as making an
investment (frequently a low-interest loan; sometimes
an equity investment) from which it expects to see a
financial as well as a social return. The new organizational structures created by entrepreneurs such as
Mark Zuckerberg, Jeff Skoll, and Pierre Omidyar are
designed to facilitate this kind of impact investing.

Foundations have other tools available besides their money. For instance, they can bring together organizations and people who don't normally talk to one another and help them to find common ground. Because foundations have their own money and generally do not have a political or financial stake in the outcome (and because people usually return their phone calls), foundations are ideally positioned to serve as "neutral conveners."

As an example, beginning in 2009, The SCAN Foundation convened a group of Washington, DC-based long-term care experts, most of whom were advancing the interests of their own organization and often saw each other as competitors. However, the members of the group shared a common interest in long-term care legislation, and as the Affordable Care Act was being debated in Congress, they met every week to discuss the practical aspects of incorporating coverage for long-term care into the pending law. In fact, the group's analyses proved to be influential when the CLASS Act, designed to provide long-term care insurance, became part of the legislation (although it was later repealed).

In another example, The Wyoming Community Foundation— recognizing that the challenges facing the state's nursing workforce were too great for any one group to solve on its own—brought together the state's nursing leaders, hospital executives, physician leaders, and state government officials in a unified collaborative effort to upgrade the training of nurses throughout the state.

Additionally, foundations can collaborate with one another to address compelling issues. Many examples attest to the influence that foundations can have when they put aside their differences and work together. In 2014, as part the so-called "Grand Bargain," the Detroit-based Community Foundation for Southeast Michigan organized an extraordinary collaborative philanthropic effort—including the Ford Foundation, The Kresge Foundation, the John S. and James L. Knight Foundation, and nine other foundations—that helped to save Detroit from bankruptcy and prevent the sale of its outstanding art collection.

And back in 1987, at the height of the AIDS epidemic in this country, the Ford Foundation spearheaded the National AIDS Community Partnership (now called AIDS United), an unusual partnership of national and local foundations that initially focused on eight communities particularly hard-hit by the epidemic. The local foundations in turn recruited additional local funders to join the partnership in their communities. In Washington, DC, for example, the Eugene and Agnes E. Mayer Foundation brought another 20 local funders into that city's AIDS partnership.

Finally, foundations can publicize ideas, findings from research, and results of evaluations. The Henry J. Kaiser Family Foundation is a good example. Its website is a go-to resource for information on health policy, its polling work is widely cited, and its in-house team of journalists produces material that is widely disseminated by the media.

Step 3. Determine priorities and goals

Foundations have finite resources. Once they understand the needs and know the resources and tools potentially available to address them, foundation leaders must make hard choices about where and how they can deploy their resources most effectively. That is, what are the priorities? We typically advise foundations that critical decisions of this kind should be discussed at a board retreat (or sometimes a series of retreats) that allows ample time for board members to consider the options away from the pressures of routine decision-making.

In making the determination about strategic priorities, a few points should be kept in mind:

Planning tools adapted from the business community can help, as long as they don't become too complicated.

These include tools such as SWOT analysis (strengths, weaknesses, obstacles, and threats), systems analysis, logic models, and theories of change.

The scope of the foundation's intervention should be commensurate with the scale of the problem. Taking the "denominator" into account is critical in order to determine what it will take to make a meaningful difference.

If there are an estimated 5,000 kids in need of drug treatment in a given community, funding a treatment program that serves

200 kids won't have much of an impact on the overall problem. While this may sound like an obvious point, in our experience it is all too often overlooked by foundations—with predictably disappointing results. We will come back to this shortly.

Foundations rarely have enough resources to solve social problems by themselves, even at the local level.

The key question is: how much of an impact are the foundation's resources—combined with those of others—likely to have? In this regard, foundations should avoid the temptation to be unrealistically optimistic about what they can accomplish. A local foundation that we worked with had set a very ambitious goal for its childhood obesity initiative. While the CEO had intended it to be a "stretch" goal that would inspire superior performance, his board took him at his word and became increasingly restive as it became apparent that the goal would not be reached. The result was a significant retrenchment in the initiative.

A foundation's goals can be stated in general terms or in specific, often quantitative, terms. Each has advantages and disadvantages.

The upside of stating its goal in general terms—such as improving access to early childhood education for low-income children—is that it enables the foundation to support a range of organizations working on a variety of issues that fall within the goal area, and so it may help to build or strengthen the field. Also, because the funded organizations are presumably using the foundation's grants to do work that they themselves really want to do (rather than trying to meet a specific target set by the foundation), they are motivated to do their best.

The downside is that while all of the grants that a foundation makes in an area may indeed help to build the field, they won't necessarily bring about change that can be measured quantitatively. This is both because quantitative targets were not set and because the grants themselves—although they all fall within the same broad goal area—are not coordinated or focused in a way that is likely to bring about quantitative change. As a result, some of the foundation's board members may become frustrated, arguing that the foundation has spent a lot of money on these general goals but that nothing has changed.

To head off this kind of frustration, a foundation may instead opt for a more specific goal with an explicit quantitative target to be achieved within a specified timeframe—for example, ensuring that at least 12,000 additional Philadelphia children enter Head Start or Early Head Start programs within the next three years. This kind of specificity has the advantage of focusing the foundation's efforts and providing a clear yardstick with which to determine whether or not progress is being made toward the goal. If it is, the board has the satisfaction of knowing that something *has* changed, and that presumably the foundation's support has contributed to that change.

However, this approach also has some potential downsides. First, other factors beyond the foundation's control may determine whether or not the foundation's goal is reached. For example, if there were to be another major recession along the lines of the 2008 crash, there could be major cuts to programs like Head Start, making the goal of adding 12,000 more Philadelphia children to the program much more difficult, if not impossible, to achieve. Second, the goal may have been chosen because it was measurable rather than because it was important (that is, the goal may have been met, but it did not make much of a difference). And third, because grantees are now working to help achieve a specific goal set by the foundation rather than their own organizational goals, they may not be as motivated to do their best. (One potential remedy might be to provide some kind of performance bonus for those grantees who achieve the specific outcomes agreed to at the start of their grants.)

Which kinds of goals a foundation chooses to adopt—general or specific—is a matter of the board's preferences and expectations, and there is no right or wrong answer. What is important, however, is that the board makes a conscious decision about the kind of goals that it wants the foundation to pursue, and that it does so with a full understanding of the pros and cons of each approach.

> Assuming that the goals were well thought out when the board adopted them, they should remain in place for a reasonable time period—five years or more. But even while the goals may remain fixed, a foundation should be flexible in the implementation of its strategy to achieve those goals.

It is also important to understand that while the foundation's staff is accountable for developing and faithfully implementing an effective strategy, it cannot be held accountable for whether or not the goals and targets set by the foundation are actually reached. The reason, as suggested earlier, is that events beyond the control of the foundation (such as a severe recession or a major political change) can influence the outcome of the foundation's strategy. As they develop the foundation's goals and strategies, board and staff members should recognize that foundations do not work in isolation and that external forces can easily disrupt or force changes in their plans.

Step 4. Develop strategies to reach the goals

If a foundation has chosen to adopt a specific goal rather than a broad priority area, the next step is to develop an explicit strategy to reach that goal. While this may sound self-evident, we have often encountered foundations that think of themselves as strategic but really aren't. They make a series of grants in the stated goal area, but the grants are largely unrelated to one another and consequently don't have the kind of collective impact necessary to advance the goal.

If the foundation really wants to achieve its stated goal, it needs to carefully consider what it will take to get there—including a realistic assessment of the barriers, opportunities, and scale of the problem—and, based on that assessment, make a series of mutually reinforcing grants that together have the potential to reach the goal. In addition, the foundation may use its convening power to bring other key players into the process, and look for opportunities for collaboration to leverage its resources.

One example of this approach is Impact Alamance, a new local foundation in Alamance County, North Carolina. With a goal of ensuring that all children in the county would enter school healthy and ready to learn—and that once in school, they would be successful—the foundation looked at the number of children entering the local school system each year and quickly realized that its own resources would at best meet only a fraction of the need. To achieve its goal of helping all the county's children would require a collective effort involving school officials, non-profit leaders, the business community, grass-roots leaders, and many others, and would need to win broad public support for investing in the county's children.

Toward this end, the foundation developed a three-part strategy that included: (a) active participation in a nationally recognized program that brings all the key players in a community together in support of a "cradle to career" initiative; (b) funding for a firm that used extensive focus group and survey research to determine the most effective language to use to win the support of the broader public in Alamance County, and then trained local leaders in the use of that language; and (c) a series of highly visible grants in support of playgrounds and splashparks that helped to meet an immediate need for recreational opportunities while at the same time positioning the foundation as an important new champion for the county's children. While it is too early to tell how successful this strategy will be, it represents the kind of strategic thinking that it takes for a foundation to have a meaningful impact on the goals it has set for itself.

Strategic vs. Responsive Grant Making

Strategic grant making enables a foundation to focus on a limited number of high priority areas, thus increasing the likelihood of its having an impact. But this approach can also close the foundation off from ideas generated by the community. After all, foundation staff members don't have a monopoly on good ideas. Being open to outside ideas enables a foundation to explore approaches that hadn't occurred to its staff and to address problems that lie outside the foundation's strategic priorities but are important to the community.

Also, because most foundations are constantly being asked to fund programs that fall outside their strategic priorities (sometimes by their own board members), having the capacity to make "responsive" grants in response to such requests takes the pressure off the foundation to pretend that such grants are in fact strategic—a pretense that can gradually undermine the integrity and effectiveness of the foundation's strategic portfolio. Beyond that, it is good public relations to make responsive grants of this kind—no small matter for a foundation, especially if it should ever find itself in troubled waters.

For these reasons, it is advisable for even the most strategic of foundations to dedicate some predetermined percentage of their grant dollars to respond to proposals that fall outside their strategic priorities. There is no "right" percentage: some foundations devote all or most of their grant-making budget to such proposals from the community; others allocate nothing. For most, however, the percentage is somewhere in between. As a general rule, dedicating roughly 20 to 30 percent of its payout to responsive grants allows a foundation to concentrate most of its funding on a few priority issues while still being responsive to the community that it serves.

> Responsive grants, as we have defined them, are not another, alternative way of achieving a foundation's strategic goals. They are conceptually different because unlike strategic grants—which further the foundation's own priorities—responsive grants address the priorities of the applicant organizations.

Implementation

Once a foundation decides on its goals and develops a strategy for achieving them, the next order of business is to implement that strategy and to monitor progress toward the goals. While foundations tend to spend a good deal of time (and often a good deal of money) developing their strategic plans, implementation frequently gets short shrift. This is unfortunate since, as Steven Schroeder, former president of the Robert Wood Johnson

Foundation, has observed, execution trumps strategy. Indeed, poor execution of a good strategy is not likely to yield positive results, no matter how many hours and foundation dollars have been devoted to its development. (Of course, good execution of a poor strategy is no recipe for success either.)

One key requirement for successful implementation is that it receives the full attention of the CEO and the board. All too often, there appears to be an assumption that, once the foundation's goals and strategies have been agreed to, implementation is largely a mechanical process that can be left to the program staff without much real discussion or follow-up. Indeed, board meetings often focus primarily on "new" business, with little time for discussion of ongoing programs. This may send a signal to the staff that program implementation is not really valued. To the extent that execution does in fact trump strategy, the staff needs to know that the foundation's leadership truly cares about and values effective implementation.

Another requirement for successful implementation, as we noted a few pages ago, is that, unless the foundation is funding a demonstration project designed to test a new approach to a problem, the scope of the intervention should correspond to the scale of the problem or unmet need. Even if it is quite large, however, the foundation may not have the necessary resources to bring about major change on its own. In fact, that is quite often the case. Even the Bill and Melinda Gates Foundation, the largest foundation in the world, does not have the resources to reach its ambitious objectives, such as lifting people in developing countries out of poverty, on its own. To implement its strategy on a scale that corresponds to the scale of the problem it is trying to address, a foundation often has to leverage its resources through partnerships with other funders and/or through advocacy directed at changing public policy. That is precisely what the Gates Foundation has attempted in many of its global health programs: it has partnered with other foundations and pharmaceutical companies, and it has supported advocacy efforts intended to increase government funding in the countries where it is working and to reduce public policy barriers to achieving its goals.

> Boards should hold a retreat at least once a year to look at the big picture, to review the state of the foundation and its environment, and to consider what is working and what is not—and why.

Foundations should be prepared to modify their implementation strategies as circumstances require. Because circumstances on the ground may change and because important lessons may be learned in the course of implementing a strategy, it is essential to stay alert and be flexible in implementation. If something isn't working right, change it! A foundation should never be held hostage to an inflexible implementation plan.

Monitoring, Evaluation, and Learning from Experience

Closely related to effective implementation is the need for careful monitoring, both of individual grants and programs and of the strategy as a whole. Are the grants meeting their specific objectives, and if not, is there anything the foundation can do to help get them back on track? Likewise, are the intermediate benchmarks for the strategy as a whole being met, and if not, are there any adjustments that the foundation needs to make—either to the strategy itself or to its timeframe—in order to achieve the desired goals? Foundations frequently rely on reports from the grantees themselves to monitor the progress of individual grants, but use existing data sources (such as government statistics) and/or independent evaluators to assess the progress of their overall strategy.

While monitoring can help a foundation determine how well its grants and programs are being implemented, it won't tell the foundation what impact those grants and programs are having or what lessons may be emerging along the way. Answering those questions will require an evaluation, which may be conducted by the foundation itself, by the grantee, or by an independent researcher.

Evaluations vary greatly in terms of their scope, rigor and cost. They may include everything from an informal qualitative self-evaluation by the grantee organization, in which the organization reports its own impressions of the impact of its grant and what it has learned along the way, to a randomized clinical trial conducted by an experienced independent evaluation researcher. In general, the more rigorous and credible the evaluation, the greater the cost and the greater the level of effort required— which means that a foundation should think very carefully about why it wants to evaluate a particular program before deciding on what kind of evaluation to support. This thinking should be done at the beginning of an initiative (or series of initiatives), rather than pasted on as an afterthought.

As a rule, if the foundation just wants a general sense of what was accomplished through its grant and is not trying to use the evaluation results to convince anyone else to support the program, an informal self-evaluation by the grantee may be sufficient. This is what many foundations do, especially with their smaller grants. If, on the other hand, the foundation wants to leverage its investment in the program by convincing the government or other funders to replicate the program on a larger scale, a more rigorous and costly independent evaluation may be required.

To take one example, The David and Lucile Packard Foundation invested several million dollars in a rigorous evaluation by Mathematica, a highly regarded independent evaluation research firm, of a model program to expand children's health insurance that it was funding in Santa Clara County, California. The positive findings from that evaluation persuaded other California counties to adopt the Santa Clara model, and ultimately helped to leverage tens of millions of dollars in federal, state, local, and foundation dollars, both in California and in other states across the country.

Interestingly, an evaluation doesn't always have to yield positive results to have a major impact. The documented failure of a particular intervention or strategy can itself serve as an important wakeup call to the field. A large-scale evaluation of an intervention funded by the Robert Wood Johnson Foundation in the late 1980's to improve end-of-life care for terminally ill patients found that the intervention had no real impact on patient care. Instead of throwing up its hands and giving up on end-of-life care when the evaluation results were announced, the foundation intensified its efforts, on the grounds that the evaluation had clearly revealed that ordinary interventions would not suffice. Moreover, the foundation actively communicated the negative results of the evaluation to the public and to the medical profession as a kind of call to arms on the issue. Together with The Open Society Institute, it then followed up with a multifaceted campaign to change deeply ingrained medical norms and values that has gradually resulted in widespread improvements in end-of-life care.

These and many other examples demonstrate the potential of evaluations to amplify the impact of a foundation's programs. In addition, evaluations—even relatively low-cost, informal evaluations conducted by the grantees themselves—can yield valuable insights and lessons to the grantees and to the foundation itself. Unfortunately, some evaluation reports—particularly those prepared by outside academics—are completed so long after the program itself has ended that the foundation has long since moved on by the time the final reports are submitted. As a result, too many potentially valuable evaluation findings languish unread in the closed-grant files of the nation's foundations.

Communications

Although some foundations consider it unseemly to publicize themselves or their achievements, a strong communications program can be a powerful tool for increasing a foundation's impact. At a minimum, it enables a foundation to let its public know what it is doing and to tell potential applicants what it will, and won't, fund. For foundations seeking to demonstrate a concept or approach, sharing results widely can spur others to replicate the program and help them avoid pitfalls. Communications can get the findings from policy analysis and research to those who can use them, such as policy makers and their staffs. Foundations can also use communications to position themselves as a go-to information resource for their fields—as The Pew Charitable Trusts have done in public opinion research and The Commonwealth Fund has done in health care policy.

In addition, a strong communications program can help a foundation build its brand with the public and the media. Having a strong positive brand can help bring attention and lend prestige and legitimacy to a foundation's work. For example, the Carnegie Corporation has funded blue-ribbon commissions on a wide range of topics over the years, all with the Carnegie name, and the recommendations of those commissions have often received front-page coverage—in large part because of Carnegie's reputation. A strong positive brand may also increase the likelihood of public support should the foundation ever become subject to criticism. This makes it a little easier for the foundation to make grants or take principled positions that might provoke opposition or generate unfavorable publicity.

The key to effective communications is the foundation's president. The president is usually the public face of the foundation—the person who represents the foundation before the media and the public, as well as before high-level audiences—and any foundation wishing to build its brand and its influence must make sure that he or she is given plenty of exposure. Since it is such a public position, a foundation president who does not have extensive prior experience with the media should receive high-quality media training.

Beyond that, effective foundations utilize the many communications tools available to them. These include:

- **A website**

  With foundations, as with almost every other organization throughout the world, the website is now the single most important tool for communicating with the public—the place that a foundation can share everything that it considers important for the public to know about it.

- **Social media**

  In recent years, social media have become almost as important a communications tool as the foundation's website. Certainly, Facebook and Twitter are now commonly used to share news and information. Other social media sites are not far behind.

- **Traditional media**

  Traditional media remain an important vehicle for foundations to communicate with the public and professional audiences. TV, radio, and newspaper interviews; tag lines on NPR; newspaper and magazine stories; and scholarly articles and op-eds by staff members can all be effective ways to reach a potentially influential audience.

- **Publications**

  Most foundations issue an annual report, often posted on the web these days. Some produce print or video reports that highlight programs and people, or publish issue briefs on matters of importance.

Beyond these tools, public appearances by a foundation's president, senior staff, and board members can elevate a foundation's visibility and credibility. In part because they have expertise but do not have an organizational self-interest in issues of concern to policy makers, foundation staff members are often called upon to testify before legislative bodies. For the same reason, they are frequently asked to serve on local boards and commissions. The challenge for many foundation leaders is to choose strategically among the myriad opportunities that present themselves so that their schedule is not completely overwhelmed.

WHAT MAKES A FOUNDATION GREAT?

Since our partnership began almost a decade and a half ago, we have advised or worked with many foundations—large and small; policy focused and community focused; urban and rural; great and not so great. In addition, we each have had many years of philanthropic experience, both as grant makers and as grant seekers. Based on our experience in the field, we have drawn up the following list of thirteen characteristics—a baker's dozen, if you will—that together, we believe, can make a foundation great:

1. Great foundations have strong leadership by the CEO, working closely with a supportive yet critical board.

The best foundations are led by a farsighted, practical, and personable leader and are marked by mutual respect between board members and the staff, especially between the board chair and the CEO. We have seen some foundations where the board completely dominated the staff—in relationships that sometimes bordered on contempt—and others where the board was little more than a rubber stamp. Neither of these situations is healthy. It falls primarily to the CEO to cultivate good relationships with the board by meeting frequently with the board chair, by involving the executive committee in important decisions, and by getting to know each member of the board (and the community advisory committee, where there is one) personally. At the same time, it falls to each board member to place the foundation's interests before his or her own (or the interests of other organizations), to care enough about the foundation to pay close attention to what it is doing, and to raise a red flag if the foundation appears to be veering off-course or is falling short of its true potential.

2. Great foundations set clear priorities.

Great foundations are characterized by the kind of clear thinking that enables them to articulate clear, understandable goals. Whether the foundation sets general goals or quantitative targets, it must be clear about what it wants to accomplish. Too many foundations fall victim to fuzzy thinking, the lure of the new-new thing, or the latest fads in philanthropy, often characterized by jargon and foundation-speak. This fuzziness, in turn, gets reflected in their priorities. Vague priorities can also result from the compromises required to gain the necessary support to move forward, both from the staff and from the board. Unfortunately, while keeping the goal vague may make it easier to find common ground, it makes it impossible to know whether the goal has in fact been achieved.

3. Great foundations understand that meaningful change can take years to accomplish, stay with their goals for the long haul, and adjust their strategies when necessary.

The best foundations recognize that, as foundations, they are uniquely positioned to take the long view, and they play to that strength, focusing on problems or issues that don't lend themselves to a quick fix. They set goals that will require at least five to ten years to achieve, and unless they encounter insurmountable obstacles, they stick with them. They monitor their progress regularly, and if circumstances change or the approach they are using doesn't seem to be working, they adjust their strategy accordingly.

4. Great foundations give high priority to implementation.

Many foundations are consumed with strategic planning, spending months and even years on it. Because of this singular focus on planning, implementation often gets short shrift. Great foundations recognize that a poorly executed plan—no matter how good it looks on paper—will not yield the desired results, and so they value and reward successful implementation at least as much as they do strategic planning and program development.

5. Great foundations concentrate on what's important.

Too many foundations get caught up in concerns about process and lose sight of the real substance of their work. While it is true that the nuts and bolts of philanthropy involves a lot of paperwork and red tape, these cannot be allowed to drive out what is really important: achieving the foundation's goals and priorities. It is something akin to Gresham's Law, only instead of bad money driving out good money, process drives out substance. This is true of boards and staff alike. Staff members often spend far too much time in unnecessary meetings and paperwork. Some boards consider every single grant request, no matter how small or insignificant. These kinds of behavior can substitute for focusing on important issues, such as where the foundation is headed, whether it is moving in the right direction, and whether its strategies are on track to meet its goals.

6. Great foundations focus externally, as well as internally.

While it is important that a foundation be well run, all too often an internal focus submerges the external. As a simple example, in many foundations, program staff members are so consumed with internal reports and meetings that they don't have time to get into the field, visit grantees, and get a sense of what's really going on. The best program officers spend at least 40 percent of their time in the field. The same over-focus on internal matters is often true of foundation presidents, some of whom spend as much as three-quarters of their time preparing for and following up on board and committee meetings. They, too, must get out of the office frequently so that they can stay grounded in the real world. In addition, all staff members should remain open to a wide range of perspectives and not limit themselves to just a few sources of information.

7. Great foundations are open to criticism and honest with the public.

Because foundations are the ones with the money, they are in a powerful position vis-à-vis their grantees—or anyone else who might hope one day to be a grantee. Accordingly, many grantees and potential applicants treat foundations with kid gloves, reluctant to risk the possibility of not getting a grant. Even supposedly independent evaluators want to please foundations by writing positive reports (often sprinkled with minor critiques to show that they are doing their job). Since foundations rarely receive honest criticism, they tend to report mainly positive results of their work and lose the opportunity to learn from their failures and shortcomings.

8. Great foundations quantify when appropriate but recognize that not everything is quantifiable.

While quantitative measurement is certainly important, the old adage, "You can't manage what you don't measure," is not necessarily true in philanthropy. Programs can succeed without being subject to quantitative benchmarks. While it is often preferable to set quantifiable targets and measure progress against them, it is not always possible or desirable. For example, the best foundations recognize the importance of investing in people—often funding them year after year—even though it is almost impossible to measure the impact of those investments in quantitative terms.

9. Great foundations understand the political, social, and economic environment.

Great foundations take stock of the social and political environment not just once—during the strategic planning process—but frequently. They realize that social change—if that is the goal—often depends on political and societal considerations. And when political, social, or economic circumstances change, they are willing to modify their activities accordingly.

10. Great foundations collaborate with others.

Foundations seeking to bring about meaningful change often cannot do the job—whatever it is—by themselves. The best foundations recognize the importance of working with others, and they seek partnerships with other foundations, government agencies, non-profit organizations, and businesses. And, very important, they treat their partners with courtesy, respect, and fairness.

11. Great foundations learn from their own past experience, as well as the experience of others.

The Spanish philosopher George Santayana famously said, "Those who cannot remember the past are condemned to repeat it." This holds true for foundations as well as individuals, yet because of periodic staff and board turnover (which results in a loss of institutional memory) and because foundations tend to focus on "the next new thing" rather than looking back, some foundations fail to learn from their own past experiences or from the experiences of others. As a result, wholly preventable errors and disappointments occur and precious resources (and opportunities) may be wasted.

12. Great foundations avoid arrogance at all levels and treat others—especially applicants and grantees—with the genuine respect and courtesy that they deserve.

Because of the inherent power imbalance between those who give the money and those who receive it, arrogance is one of the two great occupational hazards of philanthropy. As we discussed earlier, it is reinforced by the fact that very few applicants or grantees will take the risk of calling a foundation on its arrogance for fear of jeopardizing their chances for funding. Yet the reality is that neither party can function without the other: while the grantee can't operate without funding, foundations can't achieve their goals without their grantees. Foundation arrogance manifests itself in many ways: not returning phone calls or e-mails in a timely fashion, not responding to proposals for months on end, not showing up for meetings on time (or at all), or simply not listening. To address this insidious problem, the leaders of great foundations must serve as models of respectful behavior and insist that staff members do the same. In addition, the leaders of great foundations make it abundantly clear to applicants and grantees that they genuinely welcome their feedback, and that there will be no penalty for speaking truth to power.

13. Great foundations care deeply about making the world a better place for those they serve and will do everything in their power to make it happen.

The other great occupational hazard in philanthropy—besides arrogance—is complacency. Because foundations are not subject to the kinds of competitive market pressures that exist in the rest of the private sector and because they are not accountable to the public in the way that government is, it is all too easy for a foundation to coast by simply making "nice" grants and staying out of trouble—especially the kind of trouble that can come from rocking the boat. The drive to live up to its full potential and make a difference in people's lives has to come from within—from the foundation's staff and ultimately from its board, which hires the CEO and reviews his or her performance. If the board cares passionately about the foundation's mission, it will hire a CEO who shares that passion, and the CEO in turn will hire a staff that is equally fired up.

For the reality is that a foundation could tick off all of the many items that we have laid out in this book—everything from drafting its articles of incorporation to evaluating and communicating the results of its grants—and still not be a great foundation. One of the most gratifying discoveries that we have made in our many years in philanthropy is that, despite the fact that it is very easy for a foundation simply to coast and bask in the warm glow of praise that inevitably falls upon those who give away money, there are plenty of foundations out there—large, medium, and small, in all parts of the country—that truly are fired up and that really do want to make a meaningful difference in the lives of those they serve.

ADDITIONAL RESOURCES

Organizations/Websites

Boardsource (www.boardsource.org) is a national organization working to improve nonprofit board leadership. Its publications, which are available online, address many topics of interest to board members, such as *Getting Your Board to Govern as a Team, Financial Responsibilities of Nonprofit Boards*, and *Taming the Troublesome Board Member.*

Center for Effective Philanthropy (www.cef.org) has a series of research publications with titles such as *Benchmarking Foundation Evaluation Processes, Benchmarking Foundation Governance*, and *The Essentials of Foundation Strategy.*

Council on Foundations (www.cof.org) publishes online and hardcover reports and guides on specific topics such as governance, advocacy and lobbying, grants management, and conflicts of interest.

Exponent Philanthropy (www.exponentphilanthropy.org) represents small foundations. Its website provides detailed guidance on topics that include starting a foundation, grant making, tax and legal matters, and investment strategy.

Foundation Center (www.foundationcenter.org) offers a trove of materials on topics such as leadership, management, training, and transparency. Its Grantspace website (www.grantspace.org) provides useful tools, including sample documents from grant makers and grant seekers.

Grantcraft (www.grantcraft.org), a service of the Council on Foundations, provides online resources on what it calls "strategic" issues, such as leadership, field building, and spending down, and on specific topics, such as education, arts and culture, and human rights.

Grantmakers for Effective Organizations (www.geofunders.org). An organization comprising more than 500 grant-making organizations, GEO is, in its own words, "working to reshape the way philanthropy operates." Its resources provide guidance on topics such as strengthening foundation-grantee relationships, supporting nonprofit resilience, learning from evaluation, and collaboration among foundations.

Independent Sector (www.independentsector.org). Among the materials produced by the Independent Sector, a membership organization of philanthropic and charitable sector leaders, is its *Principles of Good Governance and Ethical Practice: A Guide for Charities and Foundations*, supplemented by an online resource center. It also publishes reports on topics such as strategic planning and provides case studies of foundations.

National Center for Family Philanthropy (www.ncfp.org) has an online resource center with discussion papers, sample policies, and assessment tools, among other materials.

Philanthropy Roundtable (www.philanthropyroundtable.org) publishes *Philanthropy* magazine on a quarterly basis, as well as the *Almanac of American Philanthropy*.

Books

* Paul Brest and Hal Harvey, *Money Well Spent: A Strategic Plan for Smart Philanthropy* (Bloomberg, 2008)
* Joel Fleishman, *The Foundation: A Great American Resource* (Public Affairs, 2007)
* Peter Frumpkin, *Strategic Giving: The Art and Science of Philanthropy* (U. Chicago, 2006)
* Peter Karoff, ed., *Just Money: A Critique of Contemporary American Philanthropy* (TPI, 2004)
* Waldemar Nielson, *The Golden Donors: A New Anatomy of the Great Foundations* (Transaction, 2001)
* Roger Silk and James Lintott, *Managing Foundations and Charitable Trusts: Essential Knowledge, Tools, and Techniques for Donors and Advisors* (Bloomberg, 2011)
* Thomas Tierney and Joel Fleishman, *Give Smart: Philanthropy That Gets Results* (Public Affairs, 2011)
* Olivier Zunz, *Philanthropy in America: A History* (Princeton U., 2011)

Journals, Magazines, Newspapers

* *The Chronicle of Philanthropy* (www.philanthropy.org)
* *The Foundation Review* (www.johnsoncenter.org)
* *The Harvard Business Review* (www.hbr.org)
* *The Stanford Social Innovation Review* (www.ssir.org)

Made in the USA
Monee, IL
17 June 2021